COMBAT SPORTS

BOXING

Paul Mason

W
FRANKLIN WATTS
LONDON•SYDNEY

This edition 2012

First published in 2008 by
Franklin Watts
338 Euston Road
London NW1 3BH

Franklin Watts Australia
Level 17/207 Kent Street
Sydney NSW 2000

Series editor: Adrian Cole
Art director: Jonathan Hair
Design: Big Blu
Cover design: Peter Scoulding
Picture research: Luped Picture Research

A CIP catalogue record for this book is available from the British Library.

ISBN: 978 1 4451 0720 2

Dewey Classification: 796.83

Acknowledgements:
Al Bello / Getty Images: 10, 17, 19; AP Photo / PA Photos: 27; Bettmann / Corbis: 8, 15, 26, 28; British Museum / The
Bridgeman Art Library: 4; Chartoff Winkler Productions: 20; Copyright Control / Aquarius Collection: 7; Ethan Miller /
Getty Images: 23; Fabrizio Bensch / Reuters / Corbis: 18; Jeff Gross / Getty Images: 11; Joe Klamar / AFP / Getty Images :
24; John Downing / Rex Features: 9; John Gichigi / Getty Images: 11, 16, 17; Kevork Djansezian / PA Photos: 1, 5; Mary
Evans Picture Library: 6; Nam Y. Huh / PA Photos: 13; Reuters / Steve Marcus: 22; Rex Features: 29; Rick Bowmer / PA
Photos: 25; Roberto Pfeil / PA Photos: 12; The Kobal Collection / United Artists: 14; The Kobal Collection / Warner Bros: 21.
Every attempt has been made to clear copyright. Should there be any
inadvertent omission please apply to the publisher for rectification.

Printed in China

Franklin Watts is a division of Hachette Children's Books, an Hachette UK company.
www.hachette.co.uk

CONTENTS

WHAT IS BOXING?

What do Hillary Swank, Will Smith and Russell Crowe all have in common? The answer is one of the world's toughest sports: boxing.

BOXING UP IN LIGHTS

How does boxing link the actors listed above?
- Hillary Swank played a female boxer in *Million Dollar Baby*.
- Will Smith played world champion Muhammad Ali in the movie *Ali*.
- Russell Crowe played world champion Jim Braddock in *Cinderella Man*.

An ancient sport

Boxing is one of the oldest recorded sports. There are records of boxing contests over 5,000 years ago. In ancient China, Greece and Rome, boxing was a popular spectator sport.

This image of a boxing contest on a piece of Greek pottery dates back to 336 BCE.

Boxing today

Today, people learn boxing for fitness, self-defence and competition. Many boxers are unpaid amateurs, such as those who appear at the Olympics. A few boxers are professionals and are paid to fight. The best boxers earn millions of pounds.

THE RICHEST FIGHT IN HISTORY

In 2007, Floyd Mayweather Jnr fought Oscar de la Hoya for a world title. De la Hoya earned over £22 million from the fight – even though he lost!

Oscar de la Hoya (left) and Floyd Mayweather Jnr battle it out at the MGM Grand Garden Arena, Las Vegas, USA, in 2007.

ROUND 1 — THE BIRTH OF MODERN BOXING

Until the mid-1800s, professional boxers fought without gloves. This was called 'bare-knuckle' fighting. The fights could be long and brutal.

Bare-knuckle fighting

Bare-knuckle fights lasted until one of the boxers could not carry on. One famous fight in 1788 lasted for one hour, 17 minutes! Bare-knuckle fights were popular with all kinds of people – among the crowd that day was the then Prince of Wales!

Tom Sayers (left) fought John Heenan in 1860 in what was one of the last great bare-knuckle fights.

The Queensberry Rules

In 1867, the Queensberry Rules were introduced to boxing. Many of the features of modern boxing were included in the Queensberry Rules:

* weight limits (light, middle and heavyweight)
* three-minute rounds
* protective gloves.

BOXING BY CANDLELIGHT

John L. Sullivan was world heavyweight champion from 1882–1892. To avoid police interference, Sullivan once fought a bare-knuckle match by candlelight, on a boat on the Hudson River! He went on to fight 'Gentleman' Jim Corbett in 1892 for the world title. 'Gentleman Jim' was one of the first modern boxing champions. He was so famous that his life story was later made into a movie starring Errol Flynn.

A CONTROVERSIAL SPORT

Boxing has always been controversial. There have been claims of bribery, fixed fights and that boxing is too dangerous to be allowed.

Boxing and bribery

There are many stories of boxers in the past being bribed to let their opponent win. This allowed people who were in on the secret to bet on the result of the fight – they knew in advance who would win!

Most of the opponents of Italian boxer Primo Carnera (left) were bribed to give up. When Carnera fought Max Baer, who had not been paid, he was knocked down 11 times. In the end, the referee stopped the fight.

A dangerous sport

Boxing can be very dangerous. In the past, fighters regularly died in the boxing ring. Although there are many safety measures to protect boxers today, this still sometimes happens. Some people think boxing is too dangerous, and should be banned.

Michael Watson's 1991 fight for a world boxing title left him partly paralyzed. Here, he crosses the finish line in the 2003 London Marathon. The course took him six days to complete.

"Become an electrician, a mechanic, a doctor, a lawyer – anything but a fighter. In this trade, it's the managers that make the money and last the longest."
– *Muhammad Ali, three-times world heavyweight champion.*

BOXING'S TOP MOVES: PUNCHES

There are four basic punches in boxing: the jab, the cross, the hook and the uppercut.

1 **The jab**
The jab is a fast, straight punch thrown with the boxer's leading hand. It is almost always the first punch boxers throw in a combination. It can be a way of pushing an opponent back, or stopping them coming forwards.

2 **The cross**
The cross is thrown with the boxer's rear hand. The punch starts with the hand coming up beside the boxer's chin, and is then thrown straight at the opponent.

3 The hook

The hook can be thrown with either hand. The fist follows a semi-circular path, coming into the opponent's head or body from the side.

4 The uppercut

This punch is thrown upwards, to the body or head. The uppercut can shift an opponent's body position, setting them up for another attack.

GETTING INTO BOXING

The only way to learn to box properly is to join a club or gym. There, coaches can help young boxers learn the fitness and techniques a successful fighter needs.

Finding a club

Most young boxers go to a club near where they live. If there is no club nearby, the National Boxing Association can put them in touch with one. It is important to find a club with a fully qualified coach.

These teenagers are training in a gym set up by former German boxer, Lothar Kannenberg.

At the gym

The place where boxers train is called a gym. Gyms usually
have all or some of the following:

* a boxing ring
* a speedball
* a heavy bag
* mirrors on the walls, like
  in a dance studio.

"As a kid, I didn't want to fight...
even if I won, I'd come home with a
ripped shirt and get a worse whipping
from my mother."
*Max Baer, world heavyweight
champion 1934–35.*

Amateur fighters wear protective
headgear during their bouts. Most
gyms have equipment like this
that can be borrowed.

ON THE ROAD

Boxers build up their fitness and stamina by spending long hours running on the road. They also train hard in the gym.

Running and skipping

Running and skipping are important parts of boxing training. They build up leg strength and stamina. Boxers need to be able to keep moving around the ring during a fight. If they stay still too long, they get punched!

Actor Sylvester Stallone running down a street in New York, USA. He starred as Rocky Balboa in the Rocky movies.

In the gym

The pieces of equipment boxers use in the gym all help develop different skills:

* The boxing ring is used for sparring (practice fights). These help fighters practise their skills for use in a real fight.

* Working on the speedball improves a boxer's reactions.

* The heavy bag is used for practising hard punches.

* Mirrors allow boxers to practise punches and combinations of punches.

"The fight is won or lost far away from witnesses - behind the lines, in the gym, and out there on the road, long before I dance under those lights."
– Muhammad Ali, three-times world heavyweight champion.

Muhammad Ali punches a speedball in preparation for his contest with Mac Foster in 1972. Ali went on to win the fight.

BOXING'S TOP MOVES: DEFENCE

In boxing, a good defence is as important as having good punching power. Some fighters are able to frustrate their opponents with great defence, causing them to make mistakes.

1 **Slipping punches**

Some fighters are able to twist their bodies as a punch comes towards them. This causes the punch to slip harmlessly past their head.

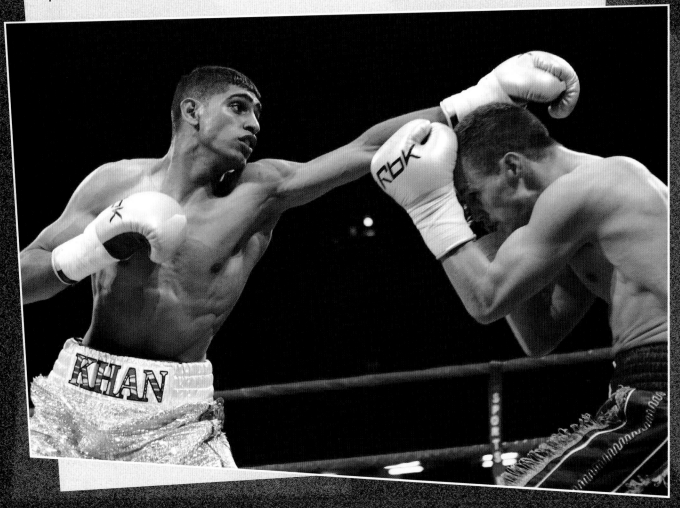

2 Blocking and parrying

To block or parry, a boxer uses his or her shoulders, arms or hands to defend against punches. A block usually stops the punch, while a parry pushes it aside.

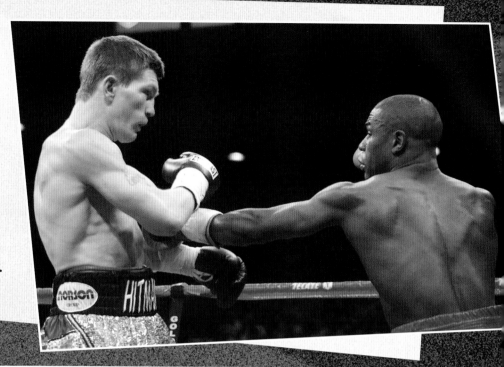

3 Covering up

Covering up is a boxer's last line of defence. The boxer covers his or her face with the gloves, and tucks his or her arms in to protect the body.

"I figured I'd find him sooner or later but I never did. I asked myself 'Where did he go?' I knew he was there because he kept hitting me." – *boxer Tony Sibson, on fighting an elusive opponent.*

MAKING WEIGHT

Boxers are divided into different weight divisions. This is a safety measure. It means they do not end up fighting someone far more powerful than them.

Nikolai Valuev of Russia (right) in his mismatch heavyweight fight with John Ruiz of the USA. Valuev's massive reach helped him win.

Weight divisions

Originally there were just three weight divisions: light, middle and heavyweight. Today, though, there are up to 17 weight divisions. They range from strawweight (under 47.6 kg) to heavyweight (over 90.72 kg).

Weighing in

Fighters are weighed before a bout, to check they are the right weight. Most fighters aim to be just a little under the maximum allowed. The weigh-in brings the fighters face-to-face for the first time. Fighters often take the chance to try and get under their opponent's skin with a few carefully chosen words.

"A good big one always beats a good little one."
– an old boxing saying.

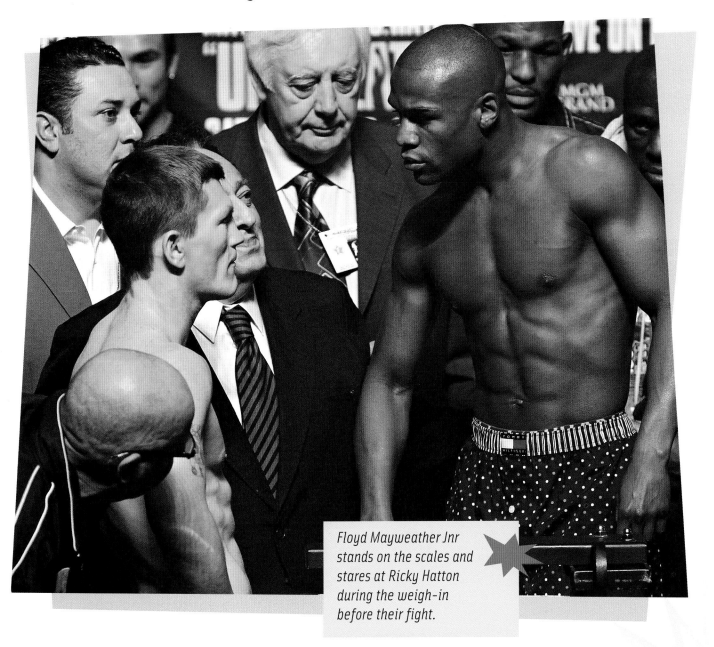

Floyd Mayweather Jnr stands on the scales and stares at Ricky Hatton during the weigh-in before their fight.

BOXING AT THE MOVIES

The first boxing movie people ever paid to see was *Young Griffo v Battling Charles Barnett*, in 1895. Boxing has been popular with movie-goers ever since.

Rocky

Rocky was inspired by a real-life bout, between Charles Wepner and Muhammad Ali. Wepner was unknown when he fought Ali, but managed to last almost the whole 15 rounds before being beaten.

Actor Dolph Lundgren (left) punches Sylvester Stallone in Rocky IV. *Five* Rocky *movies have been made so far!*

Million Dollar Baby

In *Million Dollar Baby*, Hillary Swank plays a poor waitress who takes up boxing as a way of earning money. It was the first movie to focus on female boxing, which is becoming increasingly popular.

Hillary Swank won an Oscar for her role as female boxer Maggie Fitzgerald in Million Dollar Baby.

CLINT EASTWOOD
HILARY SWANK
MORGAN FREEMAN
MILLION DOLLAR BABY

COMING SOON

Cinderella Man

Russell Crowe plays Jim Braddock, the underdog who beat Max Baer to win the world heavyweight title in 1935. Braddock became a hero to many Americans, who loved his rags-to-riches story.

"I have to believe that when things are bad I can change them."
– Jim Braddock, played by Russell Crowe in *Cinderella Man*.

COMPETITION

Most boxers train to take part in competitions. These range from contests between local clubs to Olympic and World Championships.

Amateur competition

Amateur boxers fight in two-minute rounds, and fights last three or four rounds. Each well-hit punch scores a point. The winner is: the boxer who has scored the most points at the end of the bout; or the boxer who knocks out his or her opponent.

SCORING POINTS

British boxer Amir Khan (above, left) fought Mario Kindelan of Cuba for the Olympic title in 2004 – Kindelan won. Amateur boxers score points by hitting with the white strip on the knuckles of their gloves. After winning Olympic silver in 2004, Amir Khan went on to fight professionally. Many former Olympic stars have later turned professional.

Professional competition

Today, professional fights last up to 12 rounds, with each round lasting three minutes. The winner is the fighter who wins the most rounds, or scores a knockout.

The crowd enjoys the pre-fight build up to a contest at the MGM Grand Garden Arena in Las Vegas, USA.

"I'll be glad to see him coming into the ring, because that's where it gets hard, where whatever you say doesn't mean a thing and you have to be honest and just fight."
- Lennox Lewis, former Olympic and world heavyweight champion.

BOXING AT THE OLYMPICS

Boxing has been part of the Olympics since 688 BCE, when it became part of the ancient Olympics.

The modern Olympics

Boxing was thought too dangerous for the first modern Olympics, in 1896. It made an appearance at the 1904 Games, then disappeared until 1920. Since then it has featured at every Olympics. Only amateur male boxers can fight at the Olympics.

Worapoj Petchkoom (left) of Thailand in his Olympic bantamweight fight against Guillermo Rigondeaux Ortiz of Cuba.

Weight divisions

There are 11 Olympic weight divisions, ranging from light flyweight (under 48 kg) to super heavyweight (over 91 kg).

JUDGING CONTROVERSIES

Some fights at the Olympics have ended in controversy, or argument. Some people think that the judges are not always as skilled as they should be, and that some are influenced by international rivalries.

At the 1996 Atlanta Olympics, the referee was so sure that Floyd Mayweather Jnr (right) had won, he began to raise Mayweather's arm in the air. Then he realized the judges had given the other boxer more points!

"You have to know you can win."
– Sugar Ray Leonard, 1976 Olympic gold medalist (and later, professional world champion) explains the secret of his success.

GREAT CHAMPIONS

There have been hundreds of world boxing champions. A few of them were so great that their stories have become legendary.

Joe Louis (USA)
✹ **heavyweight champion 1937–49**
American Joe Louis won the title in 1937 by beating Jim Braddock, then held it for longer than any other world boxing champion.

Joe Louis in 1936 – note the old-style boxing tunic.

"Standing across the ring from Joe Louis and knowing he wants to go home early." – *Max Baer, former world champion, with his definition of fear.*

Sugar Ray Robinson (USA)
✹ **welterweight champion 1946–51, middleweight champion 1951, 1955–7, 1958, 1959–60**
Robinson is one of the greatest boxers ever. He won the middleweight title a total of six times.

Jake LaMotta (USA)

✳ world middleweight champion 1949–51

Nicknamed 'Raging Bull', LaMotta was the first boxer to beat Sugar Ray Robinson (though he won only one of their six fights).

Joe Frazier (USA)

✳ world heavyweight champion 1970–73

Frazier is best known for a fight with Muhammad Ali in Manila, in the Philippines. The 'Thriller in Manila' was one of the greatest fights ever – Ali won when Frazier couldn't continue in the 14th round.

Mike Tyson punching his way to victory over Frank Bruno in 1996.

Mike Tyson (USA)

✳ heavyweight champion 1986–90, 1996

Tyson was the youngest ever heavyweight champion. He won the title aged 20 in 1986. His ferocity in the ring made him one of the most feared heavyweights ever.

ALI: THE GREATEST

Almost all boxing fans know who 'The Greatest' is – Muhammad Ali. Ali himself said, "I'm not the greatest. I'm the double greatest!"

Heavyweight champion

Ali won the world heavyweight title three times. He beat many of the greatest heavyweights ever, including Sonny Liston, Joe Frazier and George Foreman. One defeated opponent, Brian London, was asked if he would fight Ali again. "Sure," he said," as long as he ties a 56 lb weight to each leg."

This famous photo was taken during Ali's second fight with Sonny Liston, moments after Liston had been knocked out in the first minute of the first round.

Political activity

Ali also became famous for his political activity. He stood up for black peoples' right to be treated equally with everyone else. He also refused to fight in the US war in Vietnam, and as a result he was stripped of his boxing titles.

The crowd in Kinshasa, Zaire (now the Democratic Republic of Congo) cheer Ali before his match against George Foreman in 1974.

"I know I got it made while the masses of black people are catchin' hell, but as long as they ain't free, I ain't free." – Muhammad Ali.

GLOSSARY

amateur
An amateur boxer is never paid to fight. Only amateurs are allowed to fight in the Olympics.

bout
Contest between two fighters.

boxing ring
Area in which a boxing match takes place. Boxing rings are square, with ropes around them to mark the edges.

bribery
Paying a person to do something dishonest or illegal.

brutal
Extremely violent or cruel.

combination
In boxing, a combination is a group of punches thrown rapidly one after the other.

controversial
Causing strong disagreements.

ferocity
Fierceness and aggressiveness.

fixed
Arranged beforehand. In boxing, a fixed fight is one where one of the boxers has agreed to lose, in return for money.

knockout
Punch that knocks an opponent down so that he or she cannot continue for at least ten seconds. A knockout wins the fight.

mismatch
Fight in which one boxer is obviously far better or stronger than the other.

professional
Professional boxers earn money from fighting.

rounds
Periods of time in a boxing match when the boxers are actually fighting.

self-defence
Defending yourself against an attacker.

sparring
Practice fighting. Sparring is an important part of training for boxers.

spectator sport
Sport that large numbers of people enjoy watching.

speedball
Small, heavy ball that hangs from a low ceiling on a spring.

underdog
Person expected to lose a contest.

FURTHER INFORMATION

BOOKS

There are many instructional books about boxing, where you can learn more about some of the techniques described in this book. The only way to really learn, though, is to join a boxing club or gym.

Muhammad Ali The Life of a Boxing Hero

Rob Shone and Nick Spender
(Franklin Watts, 2007)
A biography of this world-famous boxer in graphic novel style.

Making of a Champion: World-Class Boxer

Don Wood (Heinemann Library, 2004)
Aimed specifically at young people, this book tells about the skills, techniques and dedication needed to become a boxing champion.

Inside Sport

Clive Gifford (Wayland, 2010)
A colourful informative book packed full of the facts, stats and information that you will need to follow the sport of boxing.

DVDs AND MOVIES

There are lots of movies about the lives of famous boxers. Some here are not suitable for all ages.

Raging Bull (Martin Scorsese, 1980)
Often listed by critics as one of the best movies of all time, *Raging Bull* tells the story of Jake LaMotta.

When We Were Kings (Leon Gast, 1996)
A fantastic documentary about the 1974 'Rumble in the Jungle' between Muhammad Ali and George Foreman.

On The Waterfront (Elia Kazan, 1954)
The story of a boxer who gets mixed up in a murder, this movie is famous for the line, "I coulda been somebody. I coulda been a contender!"

Million Dollar Baby (Clint Eastwood, 2004)
An amateur female boxer, played by Hilary Swank, is helped by down-on-his-luck trainer Frank Dunn (played by Clint Eastwood) to achieve her dream. Be warned though – it doesn't have a happy ending.

WEBSITES

www.wbcboxing.com and **www.wbaonline.com**
The websites of the oldest world boxing organisations (the WBA is actually the oldest), both sites list current champions.

www.abae.co.uk
Website of the Amateur Boxing Association of England features links to local clubs and boxing associations.

www.fightnews.com
An online news portal for fight fans, fightnews carries reports of the latest fights, as well as photo essays of the action.

www.olympic.org/uk/sports/programme/index_uk.asp?SportCode=BX
Section of the Olympic website that looks at boxing, featuring divisions, boxing programmes and an image gallery.

INDEX